# WOULD YOU RATHER

## GROSSOLOGY

### A GAME OF REPULSIVE AND REVOLTING QUESTIONS

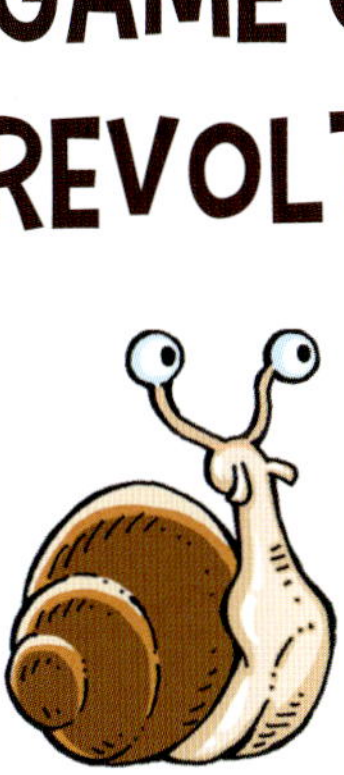

BY
**SYLVIA BRANZEI**

ILLUSTRATED BY
**JACK KEELY**

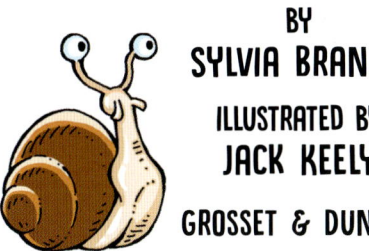

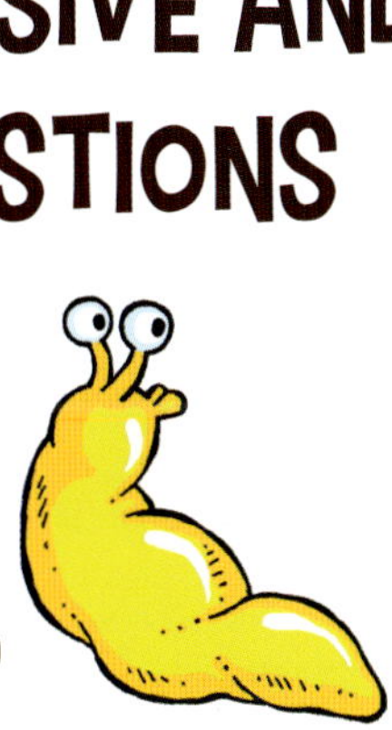

GROSSET & DUNLAP

GROSSET & DUNLAP
An imprint of Penguin Random House LLC
1745 Broadway, New York, New York 10019

First published in the United States of America by Grosset & Dunlap,
an imprint of Penguin Random House LLC, 2025

Text copyright © 2025 by Sylvia Branzei
Illustrations copyright © 2025 by Jack Keely

Penguin Random House values and supports copyright. Copyright fuels
creativity, encourages diverse voices, promotes free speech, and creates a
vibrant culture. Thank you for buying an authorized edition of this book and
for complying with copyright laws by not reproducing, scanning, or distributing
any part of it in any form without permission. You are supporting writers and
allowing Penguin Random House to continue to publish books for every reader.
Please note that no part of this book may be used or reproduced in any
manner for the purpose of training artificial intelligence technologies or systems.

GROSSET & DUNLAP and GROSSOLOGY
are registered trademarks of Penguin Random House LLC.

Visit us online at penguinrandomhouse.com.

Library of Congress Cataloging-in-Publication Data is available.

Manufactured in China

ISBN 9780593752456       10 9 8 7 6 5 4 3 2 1 TOPL

Design by Kimberley Sampson

The publisher does not have any control over and does not assume any
responsibility for author or third-party websites or their content.

THIS BOOK IS DEDICATED TO OUR FRIENDS ANNY Z AND GEORGE D, FOR ALL OF THEIR SUPERB HELP —SB AND JK

# A GROSS INTRODUCTION

So many disgusting choices to make. So many foul things to discuss with your friends and family. So many stomach-turning things to learn. *Would You Rather Grossology* is a book of four different games packed with icky information to be enjoyed by two or more players. It is perfect for the budding grossologist because you get to share your joy of learning about gross stuff.

Whether you want to get gross or be grossed out, this is the book for you. To push your edge of grossness, find other willing players and get started.

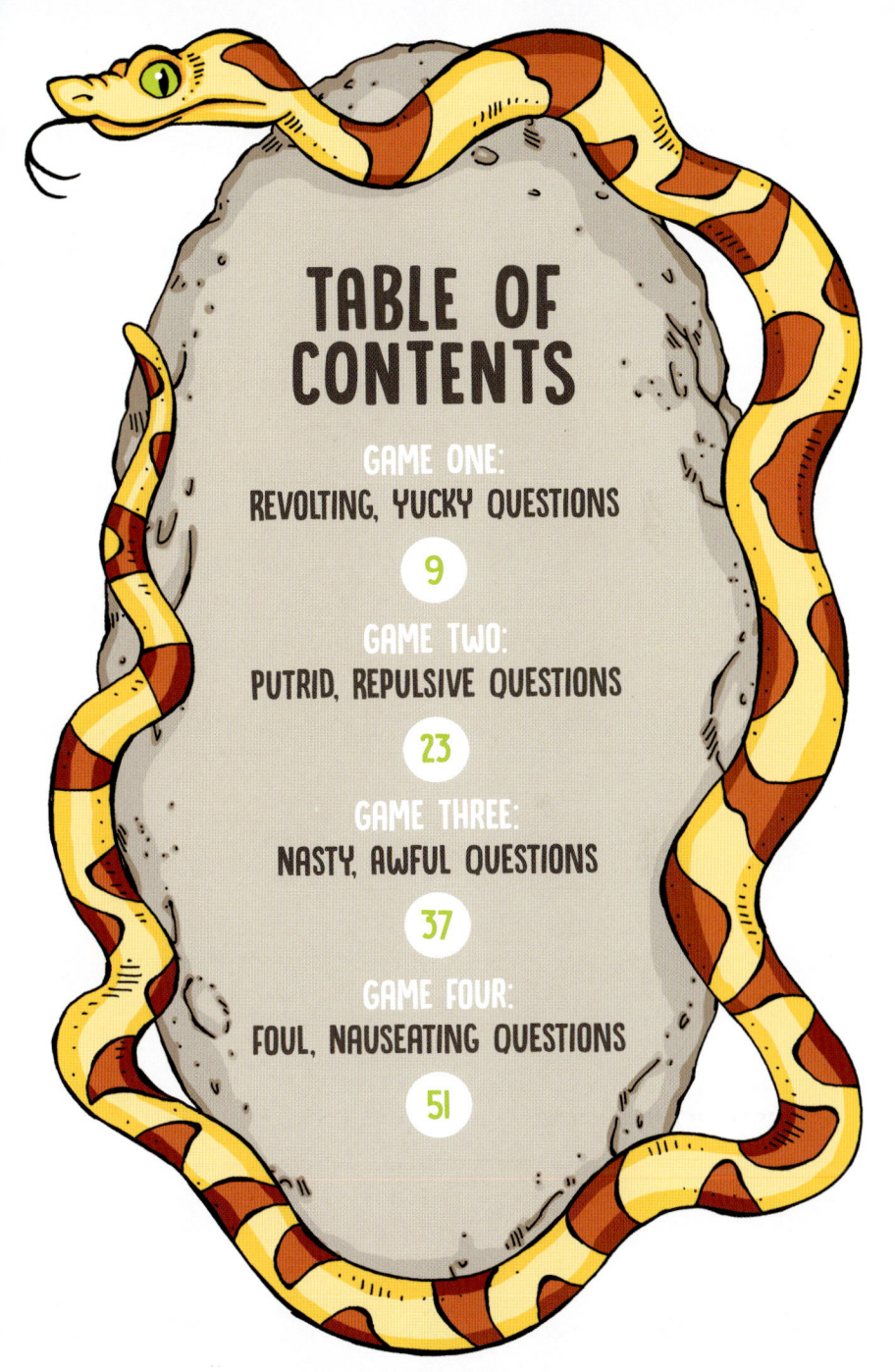

# TABLE OF CONTENTS

# HOW TO PLAY

IF YOU WANT TO KEEP SCORE, DO ALL OF THE STEPS BELOW. IF YOU DON'T WANT TO KEEP SCORE, DO ONLY THE STARRED STEPS. ★

## WHAT YOU NEED:

★ • THIS BOOK

★ • TWO OR MORE PEOPLE

• SHEET OF PAPER FOR EACH PLAYER

• PEN OR PENCIL FOR EACH PLAYER

★ 1. Choose the first reader.

★ 2. Reader asks the question at the top of the page.

3. Players write down a guess for which answer the majority of players will choose.

★ 4. Reader reads the information from the book below the question.

5. Allow players to change their guess for the most popular answer.

★ 6. Go around the table and have each player answer the question.

7. All players show their guesses. Players who guessed the most popular answer correctly get one point.

★ 8. Reader moves to the player on the right of the reader.

9. Players with the most points at the end of the game are the winners.

# GAME ONE

## REVOLTING, YUCKY QUESTIONS

### WOULD YOU RATHER LICK A TOILET SEAT OR DRINK A SPOONFUL OF KITCHEN SPONGE WATER?

- Bacteria are wee beasties you can't see with your eyes. Some bacteria are harmless. Some bacteria can make things stinky. Some bacteria can make you sick. And they live all over your house.

- A scientist researched where bacteria like to live in your house. He found they really like moist places. Your toilet seat is one of the cleanest places, with only fifty bacteria living on each square inch. Your kitchen sponge is one of the filthiest, with ten million bacteria living on each square inch.

# WOULD YOU RATHER LIVE ON A DIET OF ROASTED MEALWORMS OR FRIED TERMITES?

- You need to eat foods high in protein to help your body keep your organs and tissues in good shape. Foods high in protein include meat, eggs, dairy, beans, nuts, AND insects!

- Insects are eaten in many countries throughout the world. They are very high in protein compared to many other animal meats. And insects are very plentiful.

- Mealworms contain 4.3 pounds of protein for every twenty-two pounds eaten.

- Termites contain 4.5 pounds of protein for every twenty-two pounds eaten.

# WOULD YOU RATHER BE TASTED BY LOBSTER FEET OR BY OCTOPUS SUCKERS?

- Neither lobsters nor octopuses can taste with their mouths. Instead, they use their appendages to taste.

- Lobsters have ten legs with two ending in large claws. The two sets of legs behind the claws have hairy sensors that taste and smell the things that the lobster touches. If they taste something yummy, the large front claws grab and crush the future meal.

- Octopuses have taste and touch sensors on the surface of their suckers. It is like they have eight long fingers with tongues attached. If a sucker tastes something yummy, the octopus's many arms trap the meal in a death hug—then its rough tongues inject a paralyzing poison before the octopus eats.

13

14

# WOULD YOU RATHER CLEAN YOUR TEETH WITH ROCK SALT, MINT, PEPPER, AND DRIED IRIS FLOWERS, OR WHITE MARBLE, DATE PITS, BAKING SODA, SALT, AND PUMICE?

- The first toothpaste ever recorded was from Egypt. It was a powder of salt, mint, pepper, and iris flowers. A researcher who tried the recipe said it was a bit painful during use and his gums bled afterward, but his mouth felt fresh and clean.

- During the Middle Ages some people used a cloth to rub a powdered mixture of marble, date pits, white natron (a salty deposit containing baking soda), salt, and pumice over their teeth. After the tooth rubbing, they rinsed with wine and chewed on fennel or parsley.

16

# WOULD YOU RATHER HAVE YOUR FACE LICKED BY A CAT OR BY A DOG?

- Dogs and cats have chemicals in their spit that kill some types of bacteria and fungus. Both dogs and cats lick their butts, so small bits of poopy spit might spread to your face. This spit could contain disease-causing critters.

- Giardia, which causes diarrhea in humans, is found in 4 percent of cat dookie. Cat saliva has been connected to several other human diseases that cause severe stomach problems and diarrhea. Cat tongues are scratchy for licking clean their fur, drinking water, and removing meat from bones.

- Giardia is found in 8 percent of dog poop. Their poopy spit also contains other disease-causing bacteria. Dog saliva has occasionally resulted in people getting hookworms and roundworms. Dog licks are slimy.

# WOULD YOU RATHER BE A BODY LOUSE OR A BEDBUG?

- Bedbugs and lice are bloodsucking insects. They both feed on human blood.

- A body louse is about the size of a sesame seed. Body lice live in the bedding or clothing of infected people. The louse crawls to skin to bite and suck blood. Their bite causes itchy rashes. If a louse falls from a person or the bedding is abandoned, it will die within one or two days.

- Bedbugs are the size of an apple seed and flat. Bedbugs do not just live in beds. They live anywhere they can fit, which is basically anywhere in a room. Usually at night, they crawl out to bite skin and suck blood from anywhere on the body. A bedbug can live for several months without a meal.

# WOULD YOU RATHER DRINK A CUP OF PEE OR A CUP OF NOSE MUCUS?

- Fresh pee pee usually has very little bacteria. It is about 95 percent water and about 5 percent urea, with a tad of other stuff. Urea comes from your body breaking down proteins. New pee doesn't smell much, but once it sits around, it breaks down to ammonia. For many centuries, people have drunk urine and used it in medicine.

- Nose mucus is a slimy, thick goo that is mostly water, salts, fats, and lysozyme— a microbe-slaying chemical. Fresh mucus is crystal clear. Special cells lining your nose make a new batch every twenty minutes. Most of the goopy clean snot the nose makes is just swallowed.

# GAME TWO

## PUTRID, REPULSIVE QUESTIONS
## WOULD YOU RATHER EAT PIGS' FEET OR PIG INTESTINE?

- Pigs' feet are eaten all over the world. They can be pickled, barbecued, stewed, slow-cooked, and jellied. Pigs' feet as food are sometimes called trotters. The bones, tissue, and joints are rich in collagen, which for trotter eaters may help relieve joint pain and maintain healthy skin.

- Pig intestines are eaten anywhere pigs are raised, which means they are eaten in many nations all over the world. Fried pig intestines are called chitlins or chitterlings. Many soups are made from pig intestines. Historically, pig intestines were used for sausage casings.

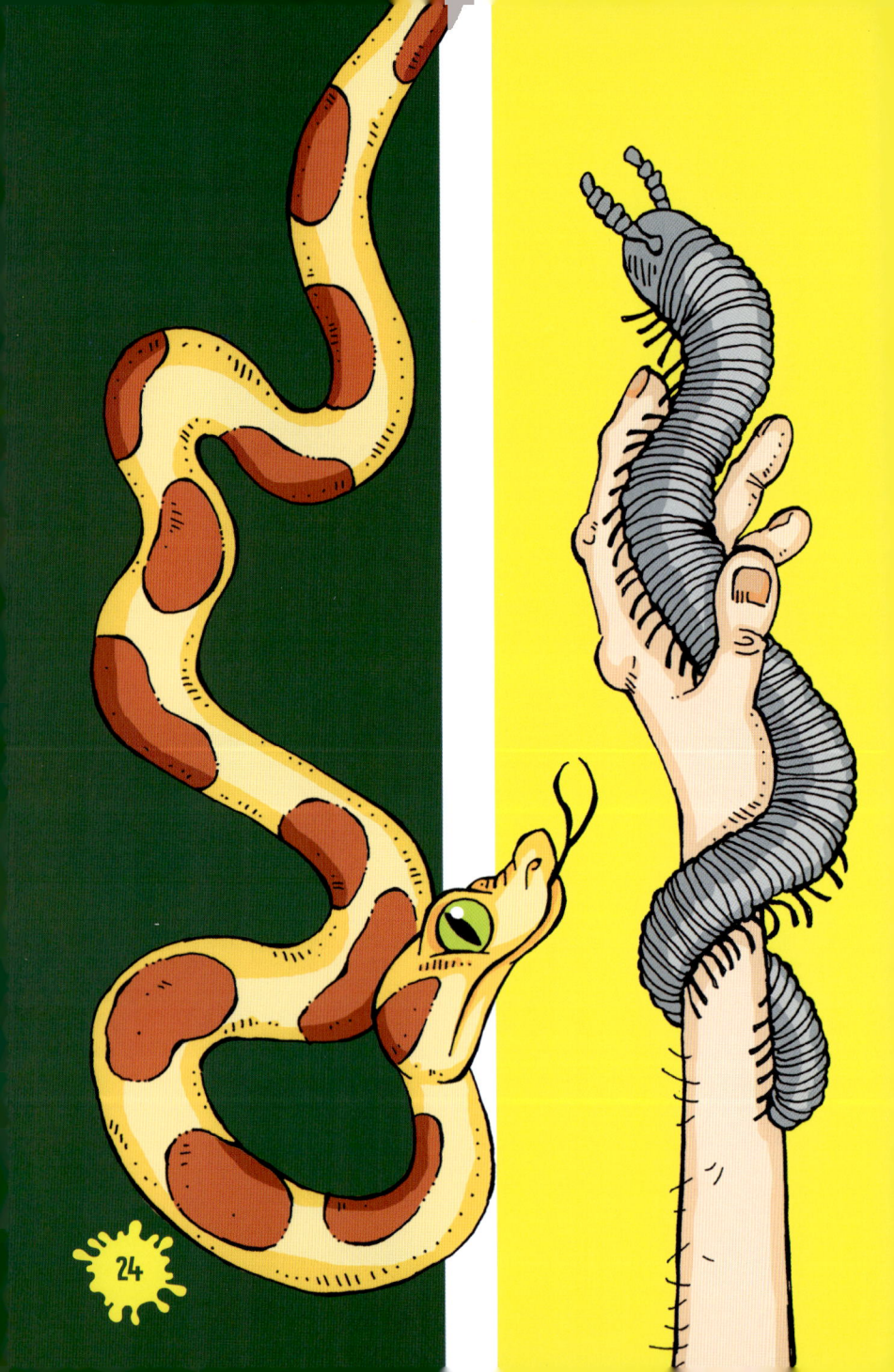

24

# WOULD YOU RATHER HOLD A RED TAIL BOA CONSTRICTOR OR A GIANT AFRICAN MILLIPEDE?

- Red tail boa constrictors are thick snakes that can grow up to nine feet long. They kill by wrapping their body around their prey and squeezing, which cuts off the blood supply. Red tail boas are not aggressive toward humans. They are a popular snake pet, but care must be taken so they don't escape.

- Giant African millipedes can get up to thirteen inches long. They have 300 to 400 legs. They are easygoing and do not mind being handled. However, when scared they can secrete a toxic substance that could irritate your eyes or mouth if you don't wash your hands after handling. They are popular invertebrate pets.

25

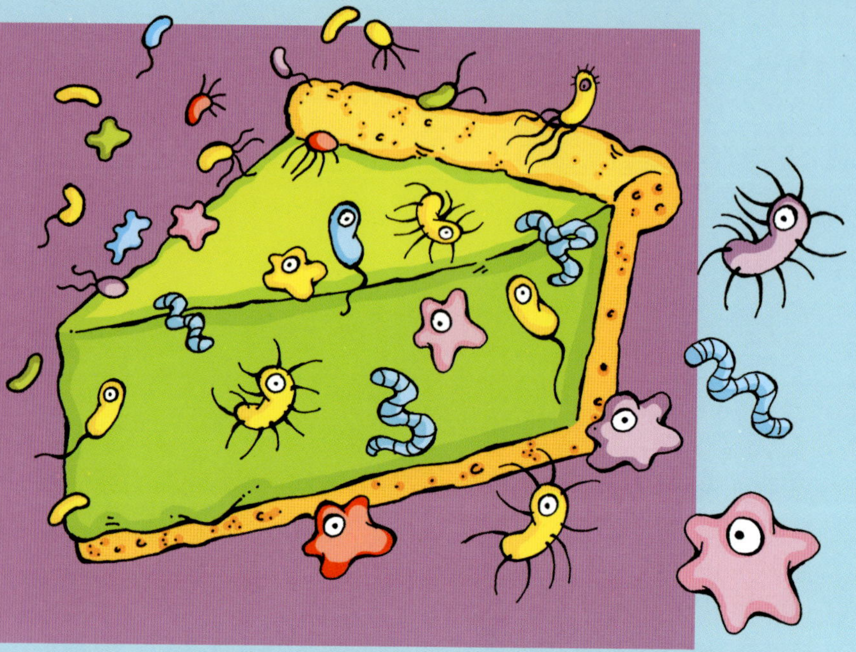

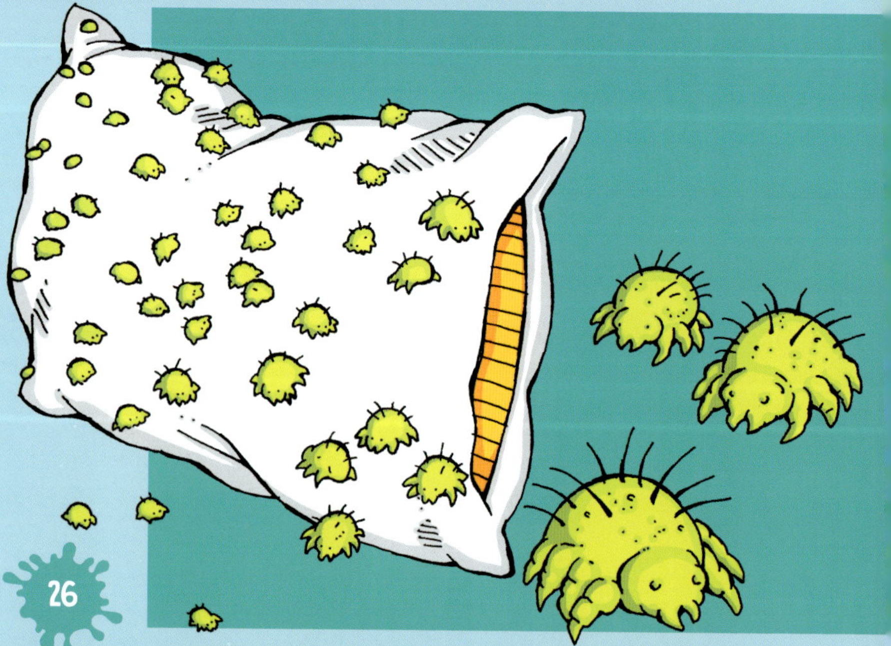

# WOULD YOU RATHER HAVE THE ABILITY TO SEE THE BACTERIA IN YOUR REFRIGERATOR OR THE DUST MITES IN YOUR BED?

- People think refrigerators do not contain bacteria because they are cold, but many bacteria can live at refrigerator temperatures. Research has shown an average refrigerator contains a population of about 1.8 million bacteria. If all spread out evenly, that would be 1,200 bacteria on every square inch.

- Dust mites are tiny insects. They munch on the dead skin cells that we constantly shed. What better place for a dust mite to live than in your bed? Anywhere from 100,000 to ten million dust mites live in a mattress. They also live, eat, poop, and reproduce in your pillows and bedding.

27

# WOULD YOU RATHER LIVE IN A HOME INFESTED WITH HOUSE FLIES OR WITH HOUSE CENTIPEDES?

- House flies are disgusting creatures. Flies taste with their feet and they are not picky eaters. They might land on and eat poop, then rotten meat, then land on your cookie. House flies eat by puking on their meal then slurping it all up. Your cookie now has poo, bacteria, and fly barf added to it. House flies spread many germs.

- House centipedes look icky. Their body is one to two inches in length with fifteen pairs of very long striped legs and two antennae. House centipedes hunt at night, so they are rarely seen. They are not aggressive. Their bite is venomous, but only slightly painful to humans. They feed on silverfish, cockroaches, spiders, and other pests.

# WOULD YOU RATHER HAVE A SNAIL CRAWL ACROSS YOUR FACE OR KISS A SLUG?

- Snails and slugs are both slimy creatures. They both ooze along on a mucus trail.

- The mucus highway allows them to travel over most everything. They are both harmless to humans. Their slime is gooey and sticky.

- Snails are slow movers. They have a single foot that secretes slime as the snail moves along. A really fast-moving snail took two minutes and thirteen seconds to travel 12.2 inches.

- A slug is basically a snail without a shell. They are fleshy blobs of goo. Tiny mites live on snails and slugs. These mites are harmless to humans.

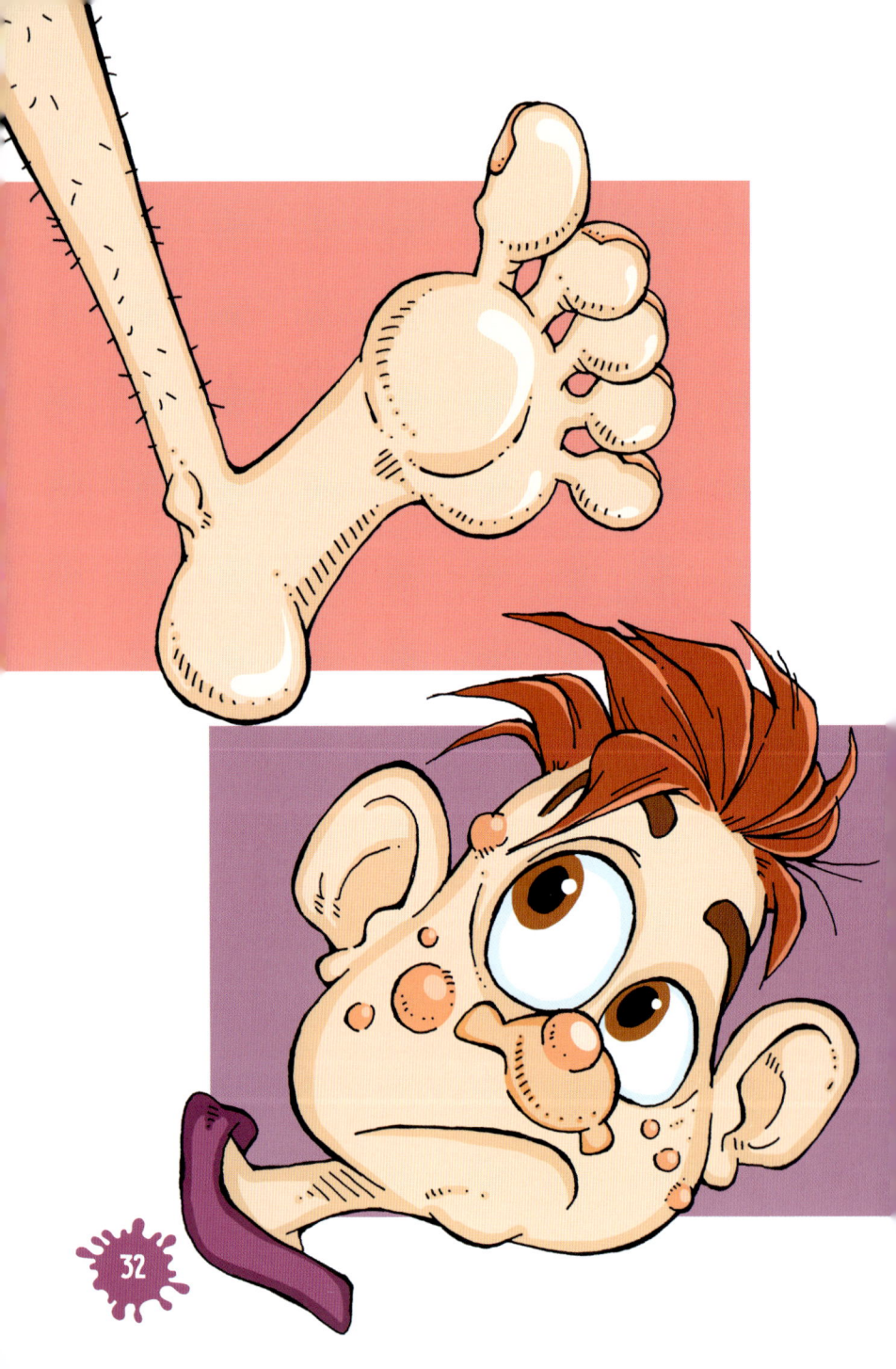

# WOULD YOU RATHER BE A PODIATRIST (FOOT DOCTOR) OR A DERMATOLOGIST (SKIN DOCTOR)?

- A foot doctor, or podiatrist, treats foot, ankle, and lower limb problems. Some of those conditions can be rather yucky, like ingrown toenails, plantar warts, thick toenails, athlete's foot, blisters, toenail fungus, calluses, and excessive foot sweating.

- A skin doctor, or dermatologist, specializes in skin, hair, and nails. The most common condition they treat is acne, or zits. Other icky problems they treat include cysts, rashes, warts, moles, eczema (scaly, itchy skin patches), skin cancers, and nail fungus.

# WOULD YOU RATHER HAVE A PET MADAGASCAR HISSING COCKROACH OR A PET RHINOCEROS BEETLE?

- Madagascar hissing cockroaches are about two to four inches long, which is big enough to cover the palm of your hand. They are laid-back and they do not mind if you hold or pet them. If they get upset, they make a hissing sound. They typically do not bite or sting.

- Rhinoceros beetles are big beetles. They can get up to six inches long—not including their long horn. They like to eat fruit. When disturbed, they can make a squeaky hissing sound. They are completely harmless. They are popular pets in many Asian countries.

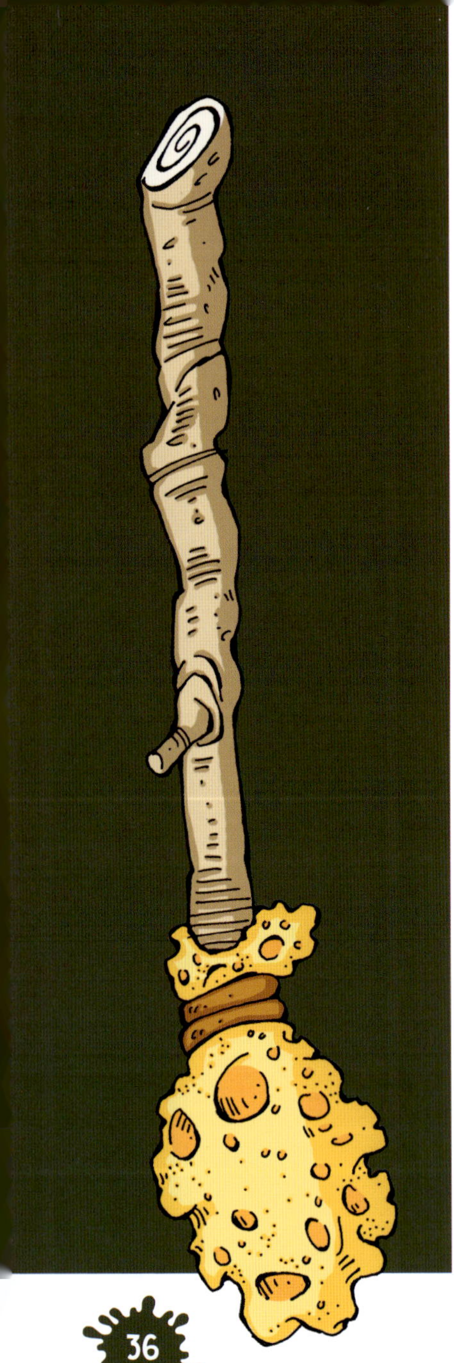

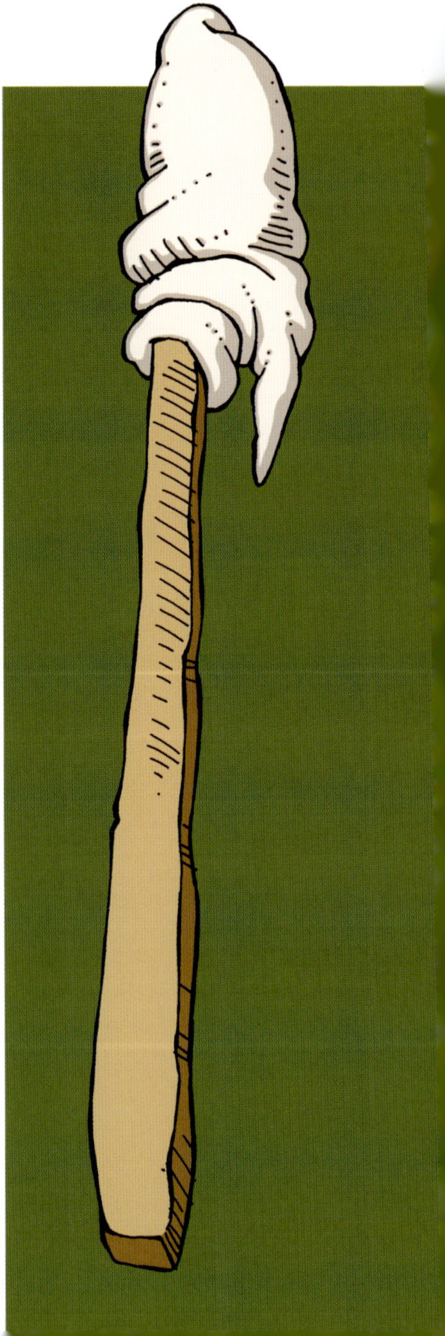

# GAME THREE

## WOULD YOU RATHER WIPE YOUR BUTT USING A COMMUNAL SPONGE-ON-A-STICK OR A REUSABLE POOP STICK?

- Roman toilets were often public outhouses with many holes. Unless you were very wealthy, people used the same sponge-on-a-stick to wipe their dirty butts. The sponge was dunked into vinegar or salt water after use for sanitizing.

- Ancient Asian cultures used poop sticks for wiping. A poop stick was shaped like a spatula. The end might be wrapped with a bit of cotton cloth. The cloth was dumped down the pit and the stick was saved for reuse.

# WOULD YOU RATHER GO WITHOUT SHAMPOO OR TOOTHPASTE FOR THE REST OF YOUR LIFE?

- There are other things you can use to keep both your hair and teeth clean.

- Shampoo alternatives work to keep your hair clean. You can use lemon juice diluted with water, apple cider vinegar diluted with water, or a baking soda and water solution followed by a rinse with apple cider vinegar.

- An easy toothpaste alternative is using a mixture of baking soda (a mild abrasive) and hydrogen peroxide (germ killer). You can add essential oils, like peppermint oil, for taste if you like.

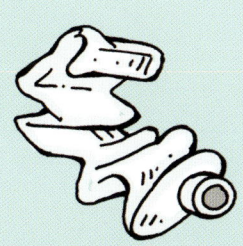

# WOULD YOU RATHER EAT EEL PIE OR ROASTED BEAVER TAIL?

- Both of these meals were very popular with American settlers in the 1700s.

- Eel pie is basically a meat pie with the meat being eels. Eel meat is a little bit sweet and it is soft and chewy. Eel pie became less popular because eels became scarce.

- Roasted beaver tail is high in fat and calories. Roasted over a fire, it has a light meat flavor, sometimes with a slight hint of fish. The texture is creamy and a little gooey. Beaver tail became less popular as beavers became scarce.

42

# WOULD YOU RATHER HAVE A DOCTOR PERFORM MAGGOT THERAPY OR LEECH THERAPY ON YOU?

- Both maggots and leeches have been used by physicians in the past. And they are being used again today.

- Maggots are the larval phase of a fly. They are little white wiggly wormlike creatures. They like to feed on decaying meat. Maggots spew out a chemical that dissolves dead and infected tissue on wounds, ulcers, and burns.

- Leeches are bloodsucking worms. Their sharp teeth slice skin. Their spit has chemicals that act as painkillers and keep blood from clotting. For thousands of years, doctors used leeching to remove "bad blood" they thought caused illness. Now leeches are mostly used after reattachment surgery, to keep blood flowing in the reattached part until the body can take over.

# WOULD YOU RATHER BE A DUNG BEETLE THAT LIVES ON POOP OR A TURKEY VULTURE THAT LIVES ON ROTTING CARCASSES?

- Dung beetles eat the doo doo of plant-eating animals like cows, camels, and elephants. They collect the poop and shape it into a ball. They then roll the dung ball to a great spot, dig a hole, and bury their yummy prize for later munching.

- Turkey vultures eat decaying meat. They only dine on dead stuff because their beaks are too weak to rip apart fresh meat. Turkey vultures have bald heads to keep the rotten meat from sticking to their heads.

# WOULD YOU RATHER TASTE MAGGOT CHEESE OR FRUIT BAT SOUP?

- Maggot cheese is also called casu marzu. It is made by placing sheep's milk cheese outside to attract cheese flies so they will lay eggs. The eggs hatch and maggots break down the cheese fats to make a soft cheese. Usually, the maggots are alive when the cheese is eaten. It has a very strong spicy taste.

- Fruit bat soup is just what it sounds like: a fruit bat boiled in a broth. While cooking, it smells strongly of urine. However, once cooked, the meat tastes like sweet chicken meat.

48

# WOULD YOU RATHER HAVE A PET TARANTULA OR A PET WEASEL?

- A pet New World tarantula is easy to care for and is easygoing. They feed on bugs once or twice a month. They live for five to ten years or longer. If you are gentle, your tarantula will not become frightened and try to bite or kick off barbed leg hairs. Their bite feels like a wasp sting, and the hairs will itch and burn.

- Weasels are cute, but they are aggressive by nature, and they are stinky. They are hunters, so they have sharp teeth and claws. They scent rub anything in their space with an oily, yellow, foul-smelling liquid from their anal sacs. If a weasel is frightened, it will release an awful stink bomb of this fluid.

50

# GAME FOUR

## FOUL, NAUSEATING QUESTIONS

## WOULD YOU RATHER DEFEND YOURSELF FROM A BULLY BY SQUIRTING BLOOD FROM YOUR EYE OR SPEWING SMELLY OIL?

- Horned lizards have a truly unique last resort method of defense. If preyed upon by a large predator like a hawk, coyote, or cat, the horned lizards squirt a stream of blood from the corner of their eye. The blood stream is actually directed at the predator's eyes and mouth.

- Fulmars are seabirds. If a fulmar is threatened, it spews out an orange-colored oil onto the attacker. They can spray the ooze up to five feet. The oil is very stinky. The oil is also very sticky.

# WOULD YOU RATHER GIVE UP DEODORANT OR FACIAL SOAP FOR A MONTH?

- Without deodorant you could just have B.O. (body odor) for a month, or you could use deodorant alternatives. You could also rub witch hazel, coconut oil, or fresh lemon juice in your pits. Or you could dust your armpits with a baking soda and cornstarch mixture.

- Without soap you could rub your face with hot water and a washcloth to get much of the grime off. Scrubs can be an alternative to soap. Some scrubs are a mush of banana and brown sugar; a mixture of honey, oatmeal or sugar, and yogurt or avocado oil; a solution of castor oil and olive oil. Rub the scrub into your face, and then rinse with water.

# WOULD YOU RATHER SMELL THE STINKIEST PLANT (CORPSE FLOWER) OR THE STINKIEST FRUIT (DURIAN)?

- The stinking corpse lily may take more than ten years to bloom, but when it does . . . *P. U.!*

- As the name suggests, the flower smells like a decaying and rotting dead body. Some folks say the smell also has a hint of sweaty socks and fish. The stink attracts carrion flies and other pollinators that like dead stuff.

- Durian is a large fruit with a spiky husky shell. When the shell is cracked open, the gagging aroma goes for blocks. People describe the smell as ripe fruit inside a teenage boy's gym sock. Researchers broke down the different smells in durian, which included honey, onion, rotten egg, caramel, soup seasoning, rotten cabbage, skunk, and fruit.

# WOULD YOU RATHER HAVE HALITOSIS (BAD BREATH) OR BROMODOSIS (SMELLY FEET)?

- Offending breath, or halitosis, is a common problem. Mouthwash and breath mints will not cure the problem but will make it more pleasant. Curing bad breath could be as easy as getting more saliva flowing by drinking fluids, chewing gum, and not mouth-breathing. Or it could be caused by a condition like an infection, which requires a visit to the doctor or the dentist.

- Stinky feet, or bromodosis, can just happen. Usually, you can just wash your feet and dry out your shoes. If hormones are changing, as in teenagers and pregnant people, feet can get foul. Foot powder or antiperspirant on the feet and breathable shoes can help. If the feet still stink, go to a foot doctor for treatment.

# WOULD YOU RATHER EAT RATTLESNAKE OR MOUNTAIN OYSTERS?

- Rattlesnake is a low-fat, high-protein meat. People say it tastes like chicken, Cornish game hens, frog legs, and even turtle. The snake is deboned, and the venom is removed before the snake is cooked. If a little bit of venom is left, it will not harm you to ingest it. Rattlesnake is eaten fried, grilled, baked, and added to stew or chili.

- Mountain oysters are not seafood at all. They are testicles from bulls, boars, and rams. Gonads are rich in vitamins and proteins. Usually they are deep-fried after the skin is peeled away and the testicles are coated in seasoned flour. Sometimes the balls are pounded flat first. Mountain oysters are often served as an appetizer or snack.

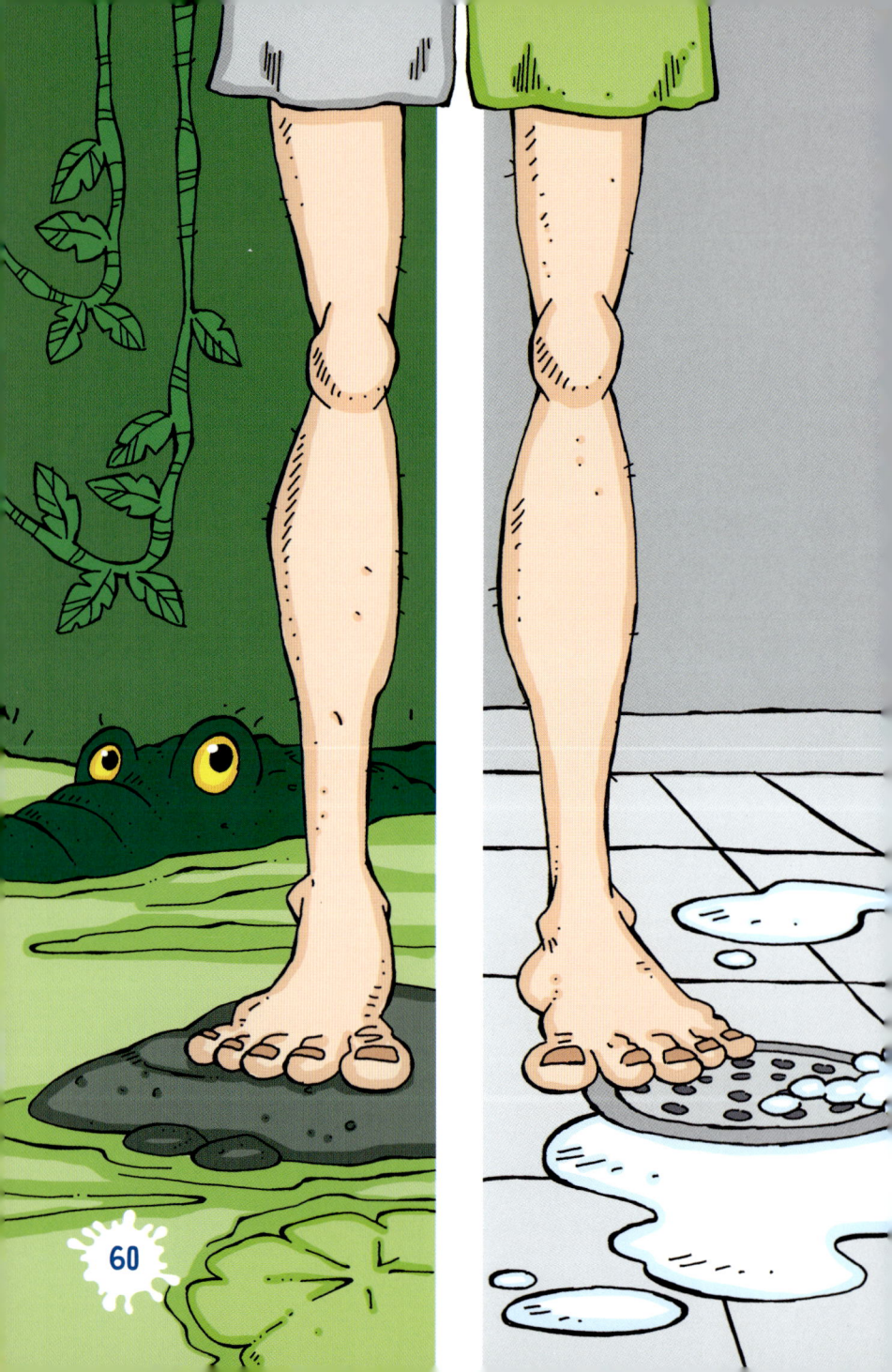

# WOULD YOU RATHER WALK BAREFOOT THROUGH A SWAMP OR A PUBLIC SHOWER?

- Walking barefoot through a swamp would definitely be mucky. The swamp mud texture can range from tomato soup to quicksand. Slow and careful steps are a must. Many animals live in swamps. Some can be dangerous, like alligators, crocodiles, snapping turtles, and water snakes. Some are just annoying, like mosquitoes.

- Walking barefoot through a public shower may seem safe—but it is not. In the moist, warm environment, unseen creatures lurk, which can cause infections. Fungi can result in athlete's foot, ringworm, and toenail infections. Athlete's foot may spread to private parts—then it is called jock itch. Wart viruses abound. Bacteria may enter through cuts. A staph bacterial infection can cause oozing blisters or worse.

# WOULD YOU RATHER BE IN A BATHROOM WHEN SOMEONE IS PUKING OR HAVING DIARRHEA?

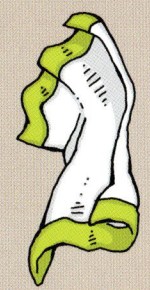

- Bodily wastes disgust humans worldwide because our body knows to avoid things that make us sick.

- Even the sound of barfing can cause some people to gag or upchuck. The vomit smell is butyric acid, formed from the breakdown of fats. Humans can detect butyric acid if the air contains only ten molecules out of a million. The other odors from puke come from stomach acids and partly digested food.

- Runny poo splattering is an awful sound. Then there is the smell. Dookie is dead bacteria, bacteria waste, undigested food, dead cells, mucus, salts, and water. Bacteria break down our foods, and stinky chemicals are produced that make poop smell disgusting. Think rotten eggs. They also make other stinky chemicals that make the poop smell disgusting.

ALSO FROM AUTHOR SYLVIA BRANZEI
AND ILLUSTRATOR JACK KEELY

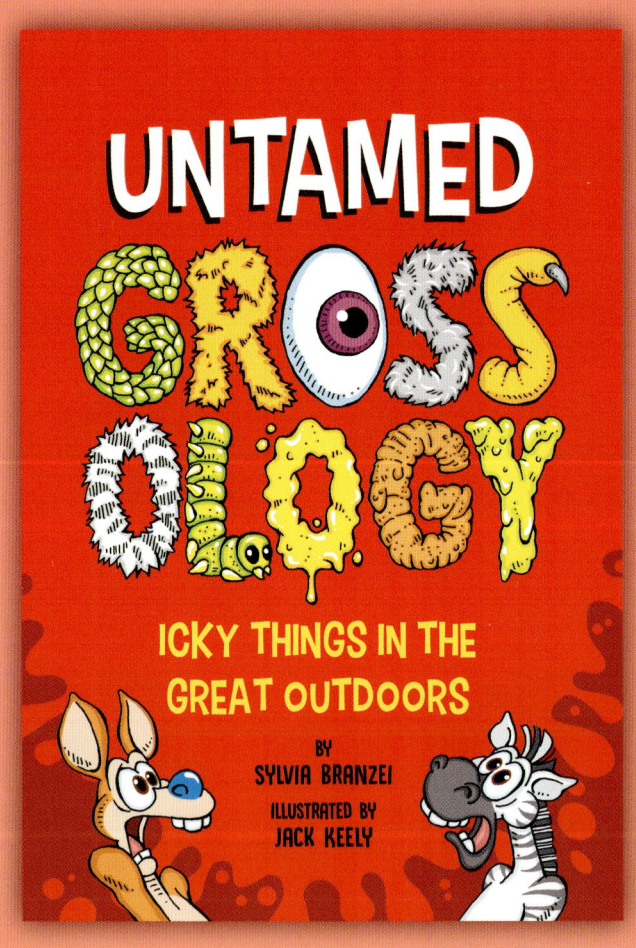

UNTAMED
GROSS
OLOGY

ICKY THINGS IN THE
GREAT OUTDOORS

BY
SYLVIA BRANZEI

ILLUSTRATED BY
JACK KEELY